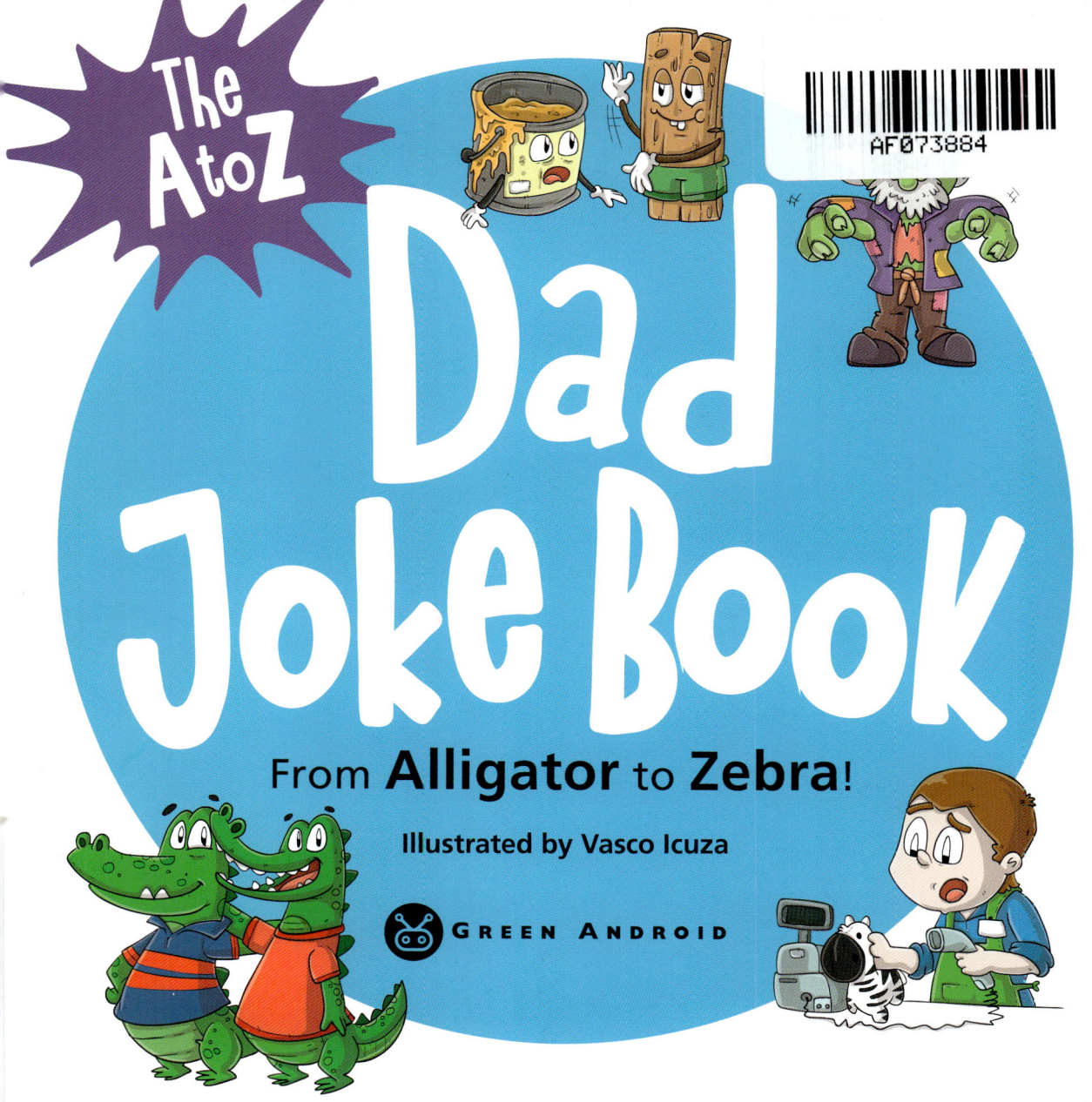

The A to Z Dad Joke Book

From **Alligator** to **Zebra**!

Illustrated by Vasco Icuza

GREEN ANDROID

The A to Z Dad Joke Book

If you love Dad jokes that are so bad that they just might be good, then this is the book for you!

The A to Z Dad Joke Book is a knee-slapping collection of over 300 groan-inducing one-liners. The jokes are ordered alphabetically, so you can chuckle your way from A to Z, or search for a joke about your favourite subject. From amusing alligators to zany zebras, the laughs don't stop!

The A to Z Dad Joke Book is all you need to tell jokes just like your dear old dad!

Q What do you get if you cross an **AEROPLANE**, a car and a cat?

A A flying carpet!

Q How many antelope live in **AFRICA**?

A A gazelle-ion!

Q What's the best **AIR** to breathe if you want to be rich?

A Billion-aire!

Q How do you tell the difference between an **ALLIGATOR** and a crocodile?

A You will see one later, and the other in a while!

Q What has more letters than the **ALPHABET**?

A The post office!

Q When does the sea get **ANGRY**?
A When someone crosses it!

Q How many **APPLES** grow on a tree?
A All of them!

Q How do you inspire an **ARTIST**?
A Easel-y!

Q Which storybook character is an **AUTHOR**?
A Little Red Writing Hood!

Q What kind of **AWARD** did the dentist receive?
A A little plaque!

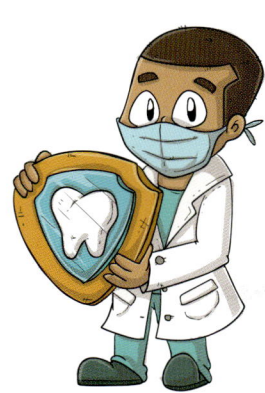

Q How is a **BABY** bird like its dad?
A It's a chirp off the old block!

Q What's the difference between a **BAD** joke and a dad joke?
A One letter!

Q Why can't you believe anything a **BALLOON** says?
A Because it's full of hot air!

Q What do **BANANAS** say when they pick up the phone?
A "Yellow!"

Q What do you call a fairy that never takes a **BATH**?
A Stinker-belle!

Q What is it called when you dream that **BEARS** are chasing you?
A A bite-mare!

Q What do you call a **BEE** that was born in America?
A A USB!

Q What do you call a **BEEHIVE** without an exit?
A Unbelievable!

Q Which **BEVERAGE** do you give a sick lemon?
A Lemon-aid!

Q Which **BIRD** is always sad?
A The bluebird!

Q Why do **BIRDS** make the best scientists?
A They already have their own beakers!

Q What do you get if you borrow money from a **BISON**?
A A buffa-loan!

Q Which burns longer: a **BLUE** candle or a green candle?
A Neither, they both burn shorter!

Q What do **BOATS** do when they're sick?
A They make an appointment to see the dock!

Q Why did the shoe fall in love with the **BOOT**?
A Because they were sole-mates!

Q What is something that has to be **BROKEN** before it can be used?
A An egg!

Q What do you get if you cross an owl with **BUBBLEGUM**?
A A bird that chews wisely!

Q Which **BUGS** like to creep up on you?
A Spy-ders!

Q Why did the **BUS** driver quit her job?
A She felt that people were talking behind her back!

Q What do you get when a pig falls into a **BUSH**?
A A hedgehog!

Q What's the easiest way to burn 1,000 **CALORIES**?

A Leave a pizza in the oven for hours!

Q How did the fruit win the **CARD** game?

A With a pear of aces!

BWAHAHA!

Q What do you call a **CARNIVOROUS** weather person?

A A meat-eater-ologist!

Q What does a **CARPENTER** eat for lunch?

A A hammer and cheese sandwich!

Q What do you get if you cross a **CAT** with a fish?

A A purr-anha!

Q Why did the **CHEF** have to stop cooking?

A He ran out of thyme!

Q What song do skunks like to sing at **CHRISTMAS**?

A "Jingle smells, jingle smells!"

Q Why is the **CIRCLE** the most ridiculous shape in the world?

A There is no point to it!

Q Why are **CLARINET** players so smart?

A Because they reed a lot!

Q Which is the **CLEANEST** state in the USA?

A *Wash*ington!

Q Why did the little **CLOUD** look up to the big cloud?
A Because it was the raining champion!

Q What do you call a **COLOGNE** for frogs?
A A frog-rance!

Q What did the **COMPUTER** say when it got new shoes?
A "I've been rebooted!"

Q Why do snakes always lose their cases in **COURT**?
A They don't have a leg to stand on!

CHORTLE!

Q What do you call a **COWBOY** who falls off his horse?
A An ow-boy!

Q What do **COWS** like to read?
A Cattle-logues!

Q How did the **CRAB** get to the ocean?
A By shell-icopter!

Q Why do nurses like red **CRAYONS**?
A Sometimes they have to draw blood!

Q What are the softest types of **CRIMES** to solve?
A Pillowcases!

Q What type of dogs are always **CRYING**?
A Chi-wah-wahs!

Q Why did the **DAD** joke cross the road?

A To get to the other sigh!

Q What do you get if you cross a **DALMATIAN** with a lamp?

A A dog that wants to be in the spotlight!

Q How do pickles enjoy a **DAY** out?

A They relish it!

Q Why did the **DEER** go to the dentist?

A It had buck teeth!

Q What kind of star is easily **DEFLATED**?

A A pop star!

SNICKER!

Q What job do **DENTISTS** do in the army?
A They're drill sergeants!

Q How do you travel across the **DESERT** without being seen?
A You wear camel-flage!

Q Why should you never eat a **DICTIONARY**?
A It'll give you thesaurus throat you've ever had!

Q What's the **DIFFERENCE** between a tennis ball and a prince?
A One is heir to the throne and the other is thrown into the air!

Q What time do clocks like to have **DINNER**?
A Ate o'clock!

Q What type of tree needs to see the **DOCTOR** regularly?
A A syc-a-more tree!

Q Where's the one place you should never take your **DOG**?
A The flea market!

Q What seems to bring everyone **DOWN**?
A Gravity!

Q What is a pony's favourite **DRINK**?
A Lemon-neighed!

Q Why are bus **DRIVERS** like trees?
A They both have routes!

Q How do canyons **EAT**?
A They gorge themselves!

Q What do a tick and the **EIFFEL** Tower have in common?
A They're both Paris-ites!

Q What do you get when you cross an **ELEPHANT** with a cake?
A Crumbs!

Q What did the Christmas **ELF** put in his shoes?
A His mistle-toes!

Q How does an **ELK** know what day it is?
A It checks its calen-deer!

Q Why did the **EMPLOYEE** get fired from the keyboard factory?
A He wasn't putting in enough shifts!

Q What do you find at the **END** of everything?
A The letter g!

Q What do you call an **EVENT** that involves money?
A An occur-rency!

Q Did you hear about the cooking class **EXAM**?
A It was a piece of cake!

Q When are your eyes not **EYES**?
A When a cold wind makes them water!

Q What do you call a **FAKE** deer?
A A play doe!

Q Why did the ghost **FAMILY** remodel their house?
A Nobody was using the living room!

Q What is a **FARMER'S** favourite thing at school?
A Field trips!

Q Which is **FASTER**: hot or cold?
A Hot. You can easily catch a cold!

Q What is a golfer's **FAVOURITE** sandwich?
A A club sandwich!

Q What do you call a monster with injured **FEET**?
A A hoblin' goblin!

Q Which game can your **FINGERS** never win?
A Thumb wrestling!

Q How do you **FIRE** a cowboy?
A Give him the boot!

Q Why didn't the **FISH** go shopping?
A It didn't have anemone!

Q Who is the **FLATTEST** superhero in the world?
A Ironed Man!

GUFFAW!

Q What did the **FLOWER** say after it told a joke?
A "I was just pollen your leg!"

Q Have you ever tried to catch a **FOG**?
A I tried yesterday, but I mist!

Q Which **FOUR** letters can get you out of trouble?
A H.E.L.P.

Q Which flowers are great **FRIENDS**?
A Rosebuds!

Q Where do **FROGS** like to store all their stuff?
A On their iPads!

Q What is a shark's favourite **GAME**?
A Swallow the leader!

Q What do you get if you cross a monster with a **GENIUS**?
A Frank Einstein!

Q What did the limestone say to the **GEOLOGIST**?
A "Don't take me for granite!"

Q Why are **GHOSTS** bad liars?
A You can see right through them!

CACKLE!

Q What is the best **GIFT** you could ever ask for?
A A broken drum. You just can't beat it!

Q Did you hear about the **GIRAFFE** and ostrich race?

A It was neck and neck!

Q Why don't mobile phones wear **GLASSES**?

A Because they have contacts!

Q What did the **GOLD** bar eat for lunch?

A Chicken nuggets!

Q What's a **GOLFER'S** favourite drink?

A Iced tee!

Q What do you get if you cross a **GORILLA** and a singer?

A A gorilla-la-la-la-la!

Q What do you call a **GREASY** insect?
A A butterfly!

Q What do you call two straws that **GREW** up together?
A Sip-lings!

Q What does a **GRIZZLY** do on a tough day?
A Just grins and bears it!

Q What do **GRUMPY** mountains have?
A Bad altitudes!

Q Why are sheep so **GULLIBLE**?
A It's easy to pull the wool over their eyes!

Q What do you call a line of men waiting to get **HAIRCUTS**?
A A barber-queue!

Q What do you get when you cross a **HAMMOCK** and a dog?
A A rocker spaniel!

Q Why was the rabbit **HAPPY**?
A Because some bunny loved him!

Q What do you call it when your **HATCHET** hits your car?
A An axe-i-dent!

Q What type of shark can **HEAL** you after it bites you?
A A nurse shark!

Q What do you call a **HEN** who counts her chickens before they hatch?

A A foolish mathema-chicken!

Q How did the eggs get to the top of the **HILL**?

A They scrambled up!

Q How did the **HISTORY** book do in the exam?

A It past!

Q How do you stop two bats from **HITTING** each other?

A Put them in a calm-bat zone!

Q What type of maths **HOMEWORK** should you always do on the sofa?

A Multipli-cushion!

Q Why is **HONEY** good for you?
A It's full of bee vitamins!

Q How did the **HOT DOG** ask the ketchup out on a date?
A He mustard his courage!

Q How come a cricket ball has a great sense of **HUMOUR**?
A It's always in stitches!

Q What type of dogs are always **HUNGRY**?
A Chow chows!

Q What do **HURDLERS** do when they lose a race?
A They get over it!

Q What happens when an **ICE** cube gets angry?
A It boils with anger, then lets off some steam!

Q How do tiny **INSECTS** escape?
A They flea!

Q What is a farmer's favourite **INSTRUMENT**?
A A harmoni-cow!

Q When do **INVENTORS** get struck on the head by lightning?
A When they are brainstorming!

Q When do **INVESTIGATORS** go to the ice-cream parlour?
A When they want to get the scoop!

Q How do you catch a **JACKET**?
A With a coat hook!

Q What do you say to a noisy **JAR**?
A "Put a lid on it!"

Q What happened when the **JEANS** completely wore out?
A They just faded away!

Q What did the **JET** think of its trip?
A It was plane ordinary!

Q Which item of **JEWELLERY** protects your valuables?
A A locket!

Q Did you hear about the couple that went to a costume party as **JIGSAW** pieces?
A They didn't really fit in!

Q When does a **JOKE** become a dad joke?
A When it becomes apparent!

Q When did the king ask to see the royal **JOKER**?
A Jest in time!

Q What do you call people who tell dad **JOKES** but aren't dads?
A Faux pas!

Q How long does a **JOUSTING** tournament last?
A Until knight-fall!

Q How does a **KARATE** teacher greet his students?
A "Hi-yah!"

Q What did the mouse say to the **KEYBOARD**?
A "You're my type!"

Q Did you hear about the **KING** who went to the dentist?
A He needed to get a new crown!

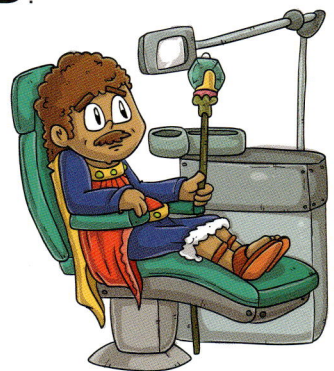

Q What did the fork say to the **KNIFE**?
A "No need to be so blunt!"

Q Did you hear about the guy who invented the **KNOCK-KNOCK** joke?
A He won the no-bell prize!

HE HE!

Q What did the **LAMB** want to be when she grew up?
A A baaa-llerina!

Q What's the least spoken **LANGUAGE** in the world?
A Sign language!

Q What sounds like a sneeze and is made of **LEATHER**?
A A shoe!

Q What has lots of **LEAVES** but never actually grew?
A A book!

Q Why was the **LIBRARY** so crowded?
A It was overbooked!

Q Why did the **LION** cross the road?
A To get to the other pride!

Q How do **LOCOMOTIVES** know where they are going?
A Lots of training!

Q Who helps pigs fall in **LOVE**?
A Cu-pig!

Q When is it bad **LUCK** to see a black cat?
A When you're a mouse!

Q What did the tree say to the **LUMBERJACK**?
A "Leaf me alone!"

Q Why wouldn't the **MAGICIANS** finish their show?
A They just didn't wand to!

Q How do you fix a broken **MALLARD**?
A With duck tape!

Q Can a **MATCH** box?
A No, but a tin can!

Q What do you call a student who hands his **MATHS** homework in late?
A A calcu-later!

Q How did the **MECHANIC** look in his new work clothes?
A OK overall!

Q What do **MECHANICS** do when they get tired?
A They take a brake!

Q What do **MICE** say when the cheese has all gone?
A "Rats!"

Q Where did the **MIST** go?
A It vanished into thin air!

Q Which type of animals live in a **MONASTERY**?
A Chip-monks!

Q What type of bird has a lot of **MONEY**?
A An os*trich*!

Q Why did the **MONKEY** go to the golf course?
A So it could practise its swing!

Q What do you call a **MOOSE** with no name?
A Anony-moose!

Q How do you get a **MOUSE** to smile?
A Say "Cheese!"

Q Why was the calendar **MOVING** so slowly?
A It was feeling week!

Q What does the **MUSICIAN** use to keep dry?
A A hum-brella!

BWAHAHA!

Q What happened to the calculator's **NEW** car?
A It got totalled!

Q Why do doors like **NIGHT-TIME** better than daytime?
A Because they are knock-turn-al!

Q What do **NINJAS** bake?
A Ninjabread men!

Q What did Pinocchio get when he blew his **NOSE**?
A Splinters!

Q Where do **NUMBERS** eat their meals?
A At the multiplication table!

Q Who keeps the **OCEAN** clean?
A The mer*maid*!

Q What do you call an **OLD** spacecraft?
A A blast from the past!

Q Which academy did the **ORANGE** attend?
A The navel academy!

Q Why was the **OX** so angry?
A Because the yoke was on him!

Q How did the **OYSTER** get to the hospital?
A In a clam-bulance!

Q What does a **PAINTER** do when she gets cold?
A Puts on another coat!

Q Would you like to hear a joke about **PAPER**?
A Never mind. It's tear-able!

Q How many friends did the bell bring to the **PARTY**?
A It brought the whole clang!

Q Why can you never win an argument with a **PENCIL**?
A Because it's always write!

Q Why do **PENGUINS** carry fish in their beaks?
A Because they don't have any pockets!

Q How does a cucumber become a **PICKLE**?
A It goes through a jarring experience!

Q What language do **PIGS** speak?
A French. Because they go, "Oui, oui, oui!" all the way home!

Q What's yellow and looks like **PINEAPPLE**?
A A lemon with a new haircut!

Q Why are pigs **PINK**?
A It's just their natural *pig*mentation!

Q Why didn't the pirate shower before he walked the **PLANK**?
A Because he knew he'd wash up on shore later!

Q What **PLANT** do you give a dad for his jokes?
A A face palm!

Q What did one **PLATE** say to the other plate?
A "Tonight, dinner's on me!"

Q What do you call a **POEM** you can read over and over again?
A A re-verse!

Q Why did the book join the **POLICE** force?
A It wanted to go undercover!

Q What does Cinderella wear on her feet at the swimming **POOL**?
A Glass flippers!

Q Why do **PORCUPINES** always win the game?
A They have the most points!

Q What did the **POT** do with the chilli's secret?
A It spilled the beans!

Q What do you call a dog that isn't **POTTY** trained?
A Puddles!

Q What do baby maths **PROBLEMS** drink?
A Formulas!

Q What do you call a **PUMPKIN** that watches over you?
A A body-gourd!

HAW-HAW!

Q How did the submarine always answer **QUESTIONS**?
A With, "I sink so!"

Q What do you call a bee that buzzes **QUIETLY**?
A A mumble-bee!

Q What do you get if you cross a **QUILT** and an eel?
A An electric blanket!

Q Why did the shrub **QUIT** working?
A It was bushed!

Q Why shouldn't you make a **QUIZ** to cheer up everyone on the hospital ward?
A The doctors do not want you to test their patients!

LOL!

Q Why are **RABBITS** constantly trying to calm down?
A Because they are always so jumpy!

Q What kind of horse **RACES** all around the world?
A A globe-trotter!

Q What do you call it when it's **RAINING** coins?
A A change in the weather!

Q What do sailors like to **READ**?
A Ferry tales!

Q What do superheroes use to mend their **RIPPED** costumes?
A Masking tape!

Q Why didn't the bread **RISE**?
A There was no knead!

Q Why are **ROBOTS** never afraid?
A They have nerves of steel!

Q Why did the **ROOSTER** go to see the doctor?
A Because he had the cock-a-doodle-flu!

Q Why can't you trust **RUBBER BANDS**?
A They always stretch the truth!

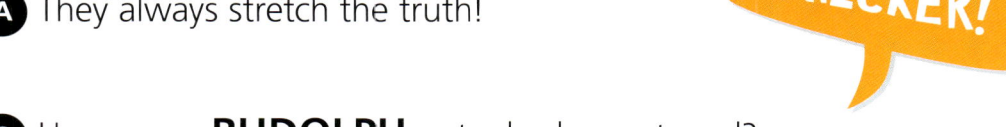

Q How come **RUDOLPH** got a bad report card?
A He went down in history!

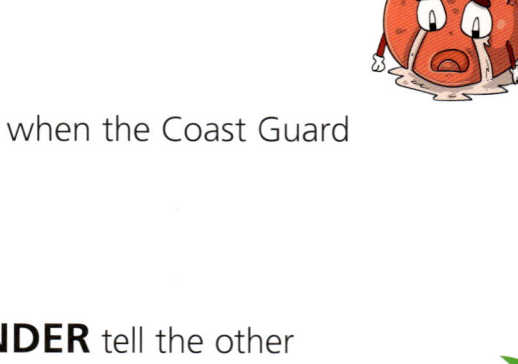

Q Why were the cherries so **SAD**?

A Because they were piti-ful!

Q What did the **SAILOR** say when the Coast Guard accused him of speeding?

A "I was knot!"

Q What did one **SALAMANDER** tell the other when he got the answer right?

A "I newt!"

Q Why did the **SANDWICH** go to the dentist?

A Because it lost its filling!

Q How much does it cost **SANTA** to park his sleigh?

A Nothing, it's on the house!

Q What's the **SCARIEST** plant?
A Bam-boo!

Q Why is it safe to tell your **SECRETS** to a sea lion?
A Their lips are always *seal*ed!

Q What do you get if you cross honey with **SHAKESPEARE**?
A To bee or not to bee, that is the question!

Q What's white, furry and **SHAPED** like a tooth?
A A molar bear!

Q How does a **SHEEP** change directions quickly?
A It does a ewe-turn!

S

Q What happened when the blue **SHIP** and the red ship collided at sea?
A Their crews were marooned!

Q What kind of **SHOES** does a lazy person wear?
A Loafers!

Q What did the **SKELETON** order with its milkshake?
A A mop!

Q Where did the snake lose its **SKIN**?
A In the shed!

Q Which is the best **SMELLING** insect?
A The deodor*ant*!

BWAHAHA!

Q How do **SNAILS** manage to get their shells so bright and shiny?
A They use snail polish!

Q What do you call it when a **SNOWMAN** throws a tantrum?
A A meltdown!

Q What makes **SONGS** but never sings?
A Musical notes!

Q Why do dogs **SPIN** in circles when they're excited?
A Because it's hard to spin in squares!

Q What **SPORT** do flowers play?
A Bud-minton!

Q What has a head and a **TAIL**, but no body?
A A coin!

Q How do you stop a shoe from **TALKING**?
A Put a sock in it!

Q Why should you do your English homework in the back of a **TAXI**?
A It boosts your vo*cab*ulary!

Q What do you get when you brush your **TEETH** with soap?
A Bubble*gums*!

Q What do you call a cow with a **TELESCOPE**?
A A star-grazer!

Q Where do **TELEVISIONS** go on holiday?
A To remote places!

Q Why aren't trees good at **TESTS**?
A They're always stumped!

Q What should you drink if you are **THIRSTY** at the dance studio?
A Tap water!

Q What **TIME** is it when the clock strikes 13?
A Time to get a new clock!

Q What does a dentist give a lion with a sore **TOOTH**?
A Anything it wants!

Q How do you find a missing **TRAIN**?
A Follow the tracks!

Q What is the cheapest way to **TRAVEL**?
A By sale-boat!

Q What type of dog can chop down **TREES**?
A A lumber-Jack Russell!

Q Why did the monkey get into **TROUBLE** at school?
A Because it was a bad-boon!

Q What do sea **TURTLES** like to study?
A Current events!

Q When do detectives carry **UMBRELLAS**?
A When they're undercover!

Q What goes **UNDERCOVER** but isn't a spy?
A Your pyjamas!

Q How did the water feel about going **UNDERGROUND**?
A It didn't take it well!

Q Who eats at **UNDERWATER** restaurants?
A Scuba diners!

Q What kind of **UNDERWEAR** is the toughest?
A Boxers!

Q Why was Frankenstein's monster so **UNHAPPY**?
A He had two left feet!

Q How does the **UNIVERSE** like its cereal?
A The Milky Way!

Q What was the thermometer doing at **UNIVERSITY**?
A Getting its degree!

Q What goes **UP** but never comes down?
A Your age!

Q If your boat turns **UPSIDE** down, can you wear it as a hat?
A Yes, it's cap-sized!

Q What do you call a very small **VALENTINE**?
A A valentiny!

Q Where do **VAMPIRES** get most of their mail from?
A Their fang clubs!

Q What did the wood tell the **VARNISH**?
A "I'm finished!"

Q What **VEGETABLE** is cool, but not that cool?
A Radish!

Q What type of **VEHICLE** is the same going forwards as backwards?
A Race car!

HE HE!

Q When is a snake glad it's not **VENOMOUS**?
A When it bites its tongue!

Q What is a grizzly bear's favourite shopping **VENUE**?
A The maul!

Q Why are cats so good at **VIDEO** games?
A Because they have nine lives!

Q What did the guitar say to the **VIOLIN** when it was worried?
A "Don't fret!"

Q What type of cities do big letters like to **VISIT**?
A Capitals!

Q What runs but never **WALKS**?
A Water!

Q What invention allows us to see through **WALLS**?
A Windows!

Q Why did the **WALRUS** feel bad about himself?
A Because he was un-tusk-worthy!

Q How do you stay **WARM** in any room?
A Hang out in the corner — it's always 90 degrees!

Q Why did the **WATCH** go on holiday?
A It needed to unwind!

Q How are most people **WATCHING** the fly-fishing tournament?

A By live streaming it!

Q What do you get when you slice a **WATERMELON** in four pieces?

A A quarter-melon!

Q What gets **WETTER** the more it dries?

A A towel!

Q What do you get if you cross a **WHALE** with an elephant?

A A submarine with a built-in snorkel!

Q What is a **WHALE'S** favourite saying?

A "Seas the day!"

Q What do you call a story on **WILDEBEESTS** coming to a screeching halt?

A Braking gnus!

Q What room has no doors or **WINDOWS**?

A A mushroom!

Q What falls in **WINTER** but never gets hurt?

A Snow!

Q What sound does a **WITCH'S** car make?

A Broom broom!

Q What's a bad **WIZARD'S** favourite computer application?

A Spell check!

Q Which month does **WOOD** enjoy the most?

A Sep-timber!

Q Where do you go to learn how to cut **WOODEN** planks?

A Boarding school!

Q What **WORD** starts with the letter t, ends with the letter t and has t in it?

A Teapot!

Q What do birds do before they **WORK** out?

A They do worm-ups!

Q Why wouldn't the **WORM** buy anything new?

A It was dirt cheap!

Q Why did the doctors laugh at an **X-RAY** of an arm?
A They found it humerus!

Q What happens if you are hit on the head by a **XYLOPHONE**?
A You may have a percussion!

Q Did you hear about the sailors who tried to make a **YACHT** out of stone?
A Turns out it was too much of a hardship!

Q Why did the **YARDSTICK** break up with the ruler?
A It just didn't measure up!

Q Why do your eyes water when you **YAWN**?
A Because you miss your bed and it makes you sad!

Q What's **YELLOW** and buzzes?
A An electronic lemon!

Q What does a **YES** person say all the time?
A I don't "no"!

Q How does a **YETI** tell time?
A With a Sasq-watch!

Q How did the **YO-YO** handle life's ups and downs?
A It bounced back every time!

Q Why did the **YOUNG** pine tree get into trouble?
A It was being knotty!

Q Why is it so difficult to sell a toy **ZEBRA**?
A It's so hard to find the barcode!

Q What did the number **ZERO** say about the problem?
A Nothing!

Q You know what I like about lemon **ZEST**?
A It has some kind of a-peel!

Q How is the **ZIP** doing?
A It has its ups and downs!

Q Why is it so hard to get through to the **ZOO** by phone?
A All their lions are busy!

HA HA!

CACKLE!

CHORTLE!

BWAHAHA!

LOL!

Published by:
Green Android Ltd
49 Beaumont Court
Upper Clapton Road
London
E5 8BG
United Kingdom

Illustrated by Vasco Icuza
Text compiled by Toby Reynolds
Edited by Shaheen Bilgrami

ISBN 978-1-912188-31-4
Copyright © Green Android Ltd 2023

All rights reserved. No part of this publication may be reproduced, stored in a retrieval system, or transmitted in any form or by any means, electronic, mechanical, photocopying, recording or otherwise without the prior written permission of the copyright owner.

Printed and bound in Malaysia, June 2023